The Captive of Fez by Thomas Aird

Thomas Aird was born on 28th August 1802 at Bowden, Roxburghshire in Scotland.

After an education at the local parish school he studied for his degree at Edinburgh University. Whilst there he became friends with fellow writers James Hogg, Thomas Carlyle and John Wilson.

After graduating Aird was encouraged to become a Church of Scotland minister but he turned down these entreaties to remain in Edinburgh and devote himself to a literary career.

His first publication was in 1826 with 'Martzoufle: A Tragedy in Three Acts, with other Poems', unfortunately the collection received little attention from either critics or the public.

Aird was a regular contributor to Blackwood's Magazine and among other works a series of essays entitled 'Religious Characteristics'.

He was best known for his narrative poem 'The Captive of Fez' which was published in 1830 to a far better and wider reception.

Between 1832 and 1833, Aird succeeded James Ballantyne as the editor of the Edinburgh Weekly Journal. From 1835, he became the editor of the Dumfriesshire and Galloway Herald, a post he then held for the next 28 years. While editor, several of his poems were published within its pages.

In 1848, he published a collection of his poetry, 'The Old Bachelor in the Old Scottish Village', which was very well received. His friend, the essayist Thomas Carlyle, said that in his poetry he found "a healthy breath as of mountain breezes."

His last published literary work was his editing of the works of David Macbeth Moir, a physician and writer, in 1852.

Aird was to now concentrate on the editorship of the Herald until he retired in 1863.

Thomas Aird died on 25th April 1876 in Castlebank, Dumfries at the age of 73. He was buried at St Michael's Church.

Index of Contents

CANTO I.

THE PRISON.

O' er golden Fez the summer sun is shining,
But not for Julian, there in durance pining.
Why thus in durance he, to whom life's spring
Was promised joy, descended of a King?
Upgrew his stately youth; up with it grew
His soul enlarged, heroic, gentle, true,
And won the honour and the love of all
Within his father's Court of Portugal
Forth then rejoicing in his early might
He rode, against the sultry hosts to fight
Of Fez, led on by black Zemberbo, far
Flashing abroad his thunder-lights of war.
O'er desert hills, and many cloudy lands,
Battling he rode, and o'er a world of sands,
The bold young Prince! He galled the Afric horde;
He won the garland for his virgin sword;
A world-wide name he'll win. Ah fatal hour!
A Captive now he's in Zemberbo's power:
Sent to the Fezzan Court, with special care
Zemberbo bade be light his bondage there;
His honour pledged that thence he should not flee,
He in the Palace otherwise was free.

But Geraldine he saw. To Abusade,
The King of Fez, was born the beauteous maid;
Born of an English mother, who had been
Raised from a slave to be the Fezzan Queen.
Her, though a playful child, that mother well
Trained up like England's women to excel,
To hold the holy Jesus far above
The Arab Prophet, and his Cross to love.
That mother died. 'Twas laid on Geraldine
At once her sportive girlhood to resign
For a grave weight of cares to be a mother
To her young sisters and her infant brother,
And make them Christians: for the King had vowed
Unto his dying wife that this should be allowed.
Nor by the Fezzan Court unfelt had been
The English manners of its honoured Queen,
That jealous law to soften which inthralls
Untrusted woman in sequestered halls.
Hence Julian saw the Princess, unreproved:
He saw and loved, and told her that he loved;
And, heart to heart, he won her gentle sigh

In thrall inglorious that his youth should lie.

But came a sterner thrall. To darkness now,
And dungeon fetters he is doomed to bow.
So wills Zenone — wild peculiar maid!
Her princely sire was slain by Abusade,
Who vengeful wrapped in one devouring roar
Of fire his palace on the Italian shore.
Perished all else within; from out the flame
Alone, unscathed, the child Zenone came.
Saved by the King, he bore her o'er the sea
To Fez, his own adopted child to be;
And chastely reared within his Court was she.
But other passions in her heart she nursed,
Of hate and vengeance, yet on him to burst.
Great was her spirit; though retired she dwelt,
Wide o'er the Fezzan realm her power was felt,
From daring counsels: for it gratified
Her soul capacious, and her native pride,
To rule; but more because it gave her power
Of wider wrath against her vengeful hour.
Thus walked she queenlike; for the Monarch still,
Soothed by her harp, indulged her passionate will,
And gave her sway, the more because he found
With large success her counsels had been crowned,
Wise from decision, nor for rashness blamed,
Though oft to fierce extravagance inflamed:
For early perils, and revengeful ire,
Repressed but cherished still, had touched her brain with fire.
She met, she loved young Julian; chaste yet bold,
Flushing in tears, her love for him she told,
Deliverance promised, waived her mighty pride,
And sought to flee with him, and sought to be his bride.
How from the Captive's just refusal burned
The Syren's heart, to equal anger turned!
Chains then for him! And he was chained and thrown
Down to a dungeon; nor the thing was known
Save by the King, who yielded his assent
To this, Zenone's ready argument: —
"What though Zemberbo speeds not to retake
Shore-guarding Ceuta, still have we a stake;
His honoured Captive shall in ward remain,
Menaced with death, till we our town regain:
His father holds, and back to us will give
The place, how gladly, that his son may live
Meanwhile our Court his durance must not learn,
So shall we shun to rouse Zemberbo stern "
To enlarge her vengeance in the Captive's ill,

Or still the purpose of her love fulfil,
That he to her, whom he had dared to spurn,
All humbly yet might be constrained to turn,
The instructed jailer, with a well assumed
Reluctance, told him that his bonds were doomed
By Geraldine, to calm the jealous pride
Of a young native prince, who sought her for his bride.

Oh, is it so? He fought against his chains,
Till worn, and sick, and sunk in fiery pains,
'Twas left him but, with nature's last endeavour,
To wade and struggle through delirious fever,
Where strength is worst disease, where manhood high
Is only fiercer than the mummery
Of palsied age, its laughter and lament,
Is but a dotage more magnificent.
No hand was there to wipe his forehead damp,
No care, no love, to trim life's fainting lamp;
Yet, helped by nature, from his bed of woes,
Subdued and soft of heart, again he rose —
Oh how subdued to think, to think that she,
His Geraldine, had doomed him thus to be!
But o'er his bosom came the stern relief
Of pride indignant, quelling softer grief,
And still his spirit, with alternate change,
From pride to sorrow was condemned to range
Revulsively, till worn, and feeling less,
And brooding more, it sunk to listlessness,
Deeming all glory gone, all hope a lie,
All life itself one dull infirmity:
And Heaven was dark, and to his spirit's tone
Even God seemed weary on his boundless throne.

II.

Thus Julian pines in durance Now has run
The yearly circuit since he saw the sun;
And, from his softening jailer, this is all
He yet has won to mitigate his thrall,
That, nightly passing from his low mid place,
One hour his steps should have a freer space
In a wide room with grated bars, that so
Heaven's breath on his young head might freshly blow
'Twas now his privileged hour; with weary pain
He paced the chamber, dragging still his chain.

But hark! near coming through the stilly night

A mandolin with touches sweetly light!
He bent to hear it: well that lay he knew,
Since oft he breathed it forth, slow sauntering through
The Palace gardens, in the twilight dim,
Till Geraldine had learned it thus from him;
Since twice, as paused his song, entranced he stood
To hear it softly back to him renewed
From her high lattice: well he knew that lay;
No time shall blot it from his heart away!

It ceased; he started; in the moonlight clear,
Outside his window, stands a lady near
'Tis Geraldine! softly he named her name,
And to his words this gentle answer came: —
"Thou good young Prince, O is it thou? The grace
Of life they shame, who keep thee in this place
Forlorn and fettered thus. Say, Captive one,
Can aught to succour thee by me be done?"

"Why, I might wish these idle days were by;
Might wish," he said, "again to see the sky
Wide o'er the world: The seasons in their range,
That come and go with sweet dividual change,
My home of early days, my friends of fame,
The camp, the field, the glory of a name,
Still haunt my heart. Yet joy, all hope, all power
Are undesired; yea death be mine this hour,
If thou hast doomed me thus! They tell me, maid,
By thee, oh thee, in fetters here I'm laid.
My soul! can it be so? Shall man believe
She comes in mockery thus to see me grieve?"

"No, no!" she answered. " But my heart, not clear
From other blame, deserves thy thought severe
For I did wrong thee, deeming, till to-day,
That thou hadst broke thy faith, and fled away
They told me so, but O it ne'er was so;
Unstained thy honour, spotless as the snow
And now, young Knight, need I declare that I
Ne'er doomed, ne'er wished thee thus abased to lie?
O no, indeed! To-day, my faithful slave
First heard of this: the news to me he gave:
Thy prison found, 'twas mine that lay to try,
To probe these depths of dull captivity;
To let thee know thou wert not all forgot,
Nor all uncared for in thy lonely lot;
To make thee hope that friends were planning for thee,
And yet again to freedom might restore thee."

"This, this is to be free; and I am free!"
The Captive murmured: " ne'er the hard decree
That chained me thus, dear virgin, came from thee!
Yon Moon in heaven how many hearts have blest,
As on she journeys calmly to the west!
She lights the white ships o'er untravelled seas,
She soothes the little birds upon the trees,
And cheers the creatures of the solitudes,
And leads the lovers through the glimmering woods,
And gives to weary hearts unworldly calm,
When slumber comes not with its wonted balm:
But not yon Moon in heaven, without a stain,
To watchful sailors o'er the trackless main,
To little birds, to desert beasts of night,
To lovers hasting by her glimpsing light,
To hearts oppressed, is, as thou art to me,
Maid with the dovelike eyes, whose grace of love I see!"

"Farewell, young Sir! From out this living grave,"
The Princess whispered, " thee I'll try to save.
Farewell, and fear not! " Geraldine is gone;
Slowly the Captive turns, and feels he is alone.

III.

Up Julian starts from slumber's broken spell,
At midnight — there's a vision in his cell!
Up from his pallet starts he: Who is she
Before him standing, beautiful to see?
Who but Zenone, in her silken dress
Of virgin white, and in her loveliness
Rarest of all those young enchantresses,
Witches of lure, wondrous, magnificent,
Whose glory for a plague midst men is sent!
" I come, " she said, " to lift thee to the day,
So thou wilt take me from this realm away,
Far to some wild free land! A bark for thee,
With white sails set upon the curly sea!
Heaven's winds, her snowy pinions how they strain!
And who but I to lead thee o'er the main;
My spirit bent to have some palmy isle
Where thou shalt reign, and I thy Queen the while?
There shall my knowledge rare thy valour aid,
And double homage shall to thee be paid
O'er the blue waves each morn canoes shall bring,
From isles around, rich presents for their King:

Peacocks, bright shells, and sweet bread from the tree,
From painted tribes thy morning gifts shall be.
Consent to this! If not, here must thou lie
Long years; if doomed not instantly to die. "
" Lady, " the Captive said, " thy hope is vain;
My love's another's, and must aye remain. "
At this, with cold and clear composure said,
How flashed the startled beauty of the maid!
She paced the cell, she stood: — " Thou shalt not live,
To her — I name her not — to her thy heart to give.
Mine shalt thou be, or nothing. From this hour
I deal with thee, for thou art in my power. "
She said, and ruffled with an angry light
From out the cell, and vanished from his sight.

CANTO II.

THE PROVOKED REBEL.

What though the failing arm of Abusade
No longer wields his battle-leading blade;
Yet still he glories in his wars, that still
To flashing victory turn his kingly will.
On Afric's north sea-border, and the coast
Of fronting Europe, gleams his dusky host,
Led by Zemberbo who still quells the bands
Of Portugal, and menaces her lands.
Thus in his palace of illumined halls
The Monarch sits, and for Zenone calls,
To see her flush beside her harp, and hear
Her intermingled song, so soft and clear,
To win his soul throughout the pleasing coil
Of varied thought without the mental toil;
For this the double joy that music gives,
To soothe the soul whilst it intensely lives.
She comes, but sits remote: See the young witch
Lean to her harp! O creature rare and rich!
Dark as the Night, but beautiful as Day,
Beautiful, lustrous dark! Wrath and Dismay
Stormed in the chords, and wailed: to fury rose
The tragic vengeance, thick with stabbing blows.
The King looked up; severe, concentrated,
Seemed coming near the creature's angry head.
Surprised he rose. But from Zemberbo came
A slave, prompt audience for that Chief to claim.

Zenone heard, and from the chamber went;
For well she guessed Zemberbo's discontent,
And would not bar it in its wrathful vent.

'Twas she who brought him thus. For when she knew
That Geraldine was striving to undo
Her Captive's fetters, and to this had pressed
The Monarch, not unmoved by the request,
Alarmed she started: what must she do now?
The King may Julian's freedom thus allow;
May still within his Palace let him live;
Nay, Geraldine to be his wife may give,
From Portugal by friendship to regain
What arms and threats of death have sought in vain:
For still the King, so well Zenone still
The matter managed with deceptive skill,
Thought Julian's sire was tried, but would not yield
Shore-ruling Ceuta up, his son from death to shield:
And thus Zenone by her arts had gained,
That still the Captive in her power remained.
But what must she do now? In secret sent,
Her hasty message to Zemberbo went
Of Julian's thrall: and much the King it blamed,
That doubly daring he Zemberbo shamed;
First, that from dungeon chains he did not spare
That Captive, heedless of Zemberbo's prayer
To treat him kindly; next that private terms
He tried for Ceuta, and Zemberbo's arms
Doubting insulted thus. Zenone well
Knew the fierce heart on which her message fell:
He'll come, he'll brave his King, away he'll go
At once a rebel, and at once a foe;
The Captive with him. Geraldine shall ne'er
Where she has failed, the wedding garment wear;
No more shall see her Knight. Zenone's hour
Of vengeance comes, as comes Zemberbo's power,
Rebellious, stern, triumphant. Well shall she
Second his arms: Eased shall her bosom be,

Eased of that King; and all his house she'll whelm,
And all his black and unbaptisèd realm.

II.

Entered Zemberbo, as the Monarch lent,
From hid reluctance, or from free consent,
Permission; wrath was on his forehead high,

Glancing like copper; from his kindled eye
Came out fierce question like a bickering sword;
And thus he stayed not for his Sovereign's word:—
"Prince Julian lies immured?—they tell me so!
I did not send him to endure this wo;
Sire, I did send him, in my battles ta'en,
In Fez an honoured Captive to remain,
Declared my kinsman, bone and blood of mine,
And far-descended of the Prophet's line.
Yet, kin forgot, be chains, be pains for him,
Let dropping dungeons rot him, limb by limb;
So thou, high King of Fez, wilt deign to show
My wish not scorned, but him a traitor foe."

"Sir Chieftain," said the Monarch, "deign to bow
The dark defiance of that servant brow!
Then haply we'll remind thee of thy boast
To win that town which rules our northern coast,
Held by the foe. Beyond thy promised date,
That Captive Prince was kept in princely state.
Thy boast was vain; it pleased us then to try
If Ceuta him from chains and death might buy.
Not bought, he dies: 'twere well he died this hour,
Just to remind thee of our sovereign power."

He said, and clapped his hands; a giant band
Of negroes come, and round Zemberbo stand.

Yet dauntless stood the Chief, and eyed his King,
Then proudly turned and scanned the sable ring:
Towering he rose as o'er the warlike brunt;
And darker grew his high embattled front;
And flashed his eye, as brings the steely dint
Red seeds of fire from the deforcèd flint.
"Me menace not," hoarse whispered he, "proud King;
A thousand hearts are ready forth to spring,
To turn my death to vengeance: ere I came
From out my camp that Captive boy to claim
(For in the distant battle I had heard
Myself despised in him thus doomed to ward),
In my great Captains' hearts I breathed my fear,
And won their oath to avenge me injured here,
To avenge that Captive too. But, Sire, no more
Of this; still let me battle on the shore;
With loyal war I've warred to take that town,
And, trust me, I shall yet restore it to thy Crown.
Around it, flashing down the coast, of all
Bravest, careers the King of Portugal,

With vigour like the eagle's youth renewed,
Has baffled me awhile, yet shall he be subdued.
Deign, Sire, still send me to the embattled line;
Thine be the conquests, but that Captive mine."
Zemberbo thus. Pausing the Monarch sate:
He longed to close with scorn the bold debate,
But feared a foe in one so stern and great;
So, feigning frankness in his voice and eye,
Thus to his rankling heart he gave the lie:—
"Why, what a jest is here! our Man of might
Deigning to pray us for one Captive Knight,—
The Man of our right hand, the Man whose name
To Fez is safety, and to Fez is fame!

Go to thy palace, Chief; the Captive there
Shall come to thee, released: those chains had ne'er
Been put upon him, had we deemed that he
Was honoured farther in thy thoughts to be.
Rest thee the night, come back to us at morn,
One day thy presence must our Court adorn;
Then haste to war, and take the wished-for town;
And be thou still the glory of our Crown."

III.

How sweetly sleeps, delivered from his thrall,
The Captive Julian in Zemberbo's hall!
For, in his dream, he hears the boys at play
On Lisbon's streets, and evening roundelay,
To whose blithe spiriting the olive maids
Of Tagus dance beneath the chestnut shades.
Slowly Zemberbo entered; drawing near
The youth, he touched and roused him with his spear.
Then called his guards: "Guards, do our wish!—But hold!
What mean these cries without? By Allah! they are bold!
Again? What ho! my arms! Each man his blade!
Bela, look forth and say what means the mad parade."

IV.

Thus they within. Meanwhile a mob without
Around Zemberbo's palace fiercely shout,
Roused by Zenone's arts: she caused the thing
Be done, as if commissioned by the King,
Who feared the Chief, a traitor: and she made
The rabble roar, as if they lent their aid

Unto their King. All this was done that so
Zemberbo's heart might to rebellion grow.
Thus rage the populace: o'er the swarthy host,
Swayed to and fro, the fiery brands are tossed.
"Allah be praised! the traitor-den's aloof
From other homes; up with them to the roof,
Up with your torches! So! The King has doomed
The rebel thus to be with fire consumed."
Such was the cry: And many a brand was flung,
And seized the palace with its flaming tongue.
"Down with the traitor!" yell they, as they spy
Zemberbo glaring from his lattice high:
Terrible glaring out, from side to side
Far stretching he looked out. "Down with him!" cried
A thousand voices. Back the Chieftain sprung.
Below, his doors were widely open flung.
Borne through the entrance crowding numbers press;
But turned the foremost from a stern redress,
Back screaming turned, rolled back the fickle wave,
And to the light their hideous quittance gave:
Eyes gashed across, bones of the brow laid bare,
Noseless and earless heads the work declare
Of swords within: Fast fled the suffering brood
Howling, and as they howled their mouths were filled with blood.
Scarce conscious, sympathetic, back dismayed
That sea of umbered visages was swayed.
Save! save! for lo! forth flashing, coming on,
Like Eblis darkly from his blazing throne,
Strides stern Zemberbo, drives the human rack,
His sable globe of warriors at his back
Round Julian, onward to the central square
Of Fez: their haughty station shall be there.
And round the Captive firmly, mutely stood
The warrior troop, and faced the multitude:
For rallying, circling, wavering, serrated
With hollowed far-retiring flaws of dread
And bold abutments of vindictive rage,
Anew the mob their warfare 'gan to wage.
In dark concentric orbit round his band
Slow stalked Zemberbo, scimitar in hand;
Slow, sternly silent: with his front of war
He faced his foes, and kept them faint and far.

Thus passed the hours till, bravely kept at bay,
The angry rout began to melt away.
Raising his sword, the Chieftain waved it round,
Then stooped, and with it wrote upon the ground
(His aspect lightening with a savage glee,

Like stormy sunburst on the darkened sea)
Short notes of desolation—war, blood, fire,
Captivity to child, to wife, to sire.
"So be ye read at morn, and on to noon,"
He said, "my lessons, to be bettered soon!
We thank thee, Abusade, for hearts resolved,
And work, half dreamt of, on our swords devolved!
Guards, do our wish: be prompt: the dawning hour
Must see us far beyond the tyrant's power."

Ere ceased the Chief, his sable men had bound
The Captive's eyes, and borne him from the ground.

CANTO III.

MOTHER AND SON.

The Captive's eyes are freed. A corridor
Has brought the party to a guarded door,
Guarded by eunuch slaves. But hark! within
A lady singing to her mandolin:
Swell the soul's bursts, the sweet relapses die.
Moved was the swarthy Chieftain to a sigh.
His nod won prompt admittance: by the hand
He took the Captive from his pausing band,
And led him in. Alone a lady sate,
Of faded beauty, darkly delicate;
Downcast her eyes; upon her hand she leant
Her cheek of sorrow: for the song was spent.
"Zara!" the Chieftain said, "dear sister-twin!
Heed'st thou not me? Must I no welcome win?"
How started she! how to her brother sprung she,
Naming his name! how to his bosom clung she!
Soft to her couch he led her by the hand,
There made her sit, and there her face he fondly scanned.
"Ay, look at me," she said; "long years have done thenpart,
And the deep shares of grief have ploughed this brow and heart.
But grief nor years have hurt my love for thee,
Nor thou severe—oh, how severe to me!
No, no, indeed! I'll call thee not severe!
Come to this heart, my brother ever dear!
O thou twin-being of my life! can I
Forget thy love for me so pure and high,
In our young days? Our kindred early lost,
Mine all thou wert, and in thyself a host!
All later sorrows, lo! they're past away,

For thou art come to live with me for aye."

"No," said Zemberbo: "Not for Fez alone
Have been my battles, to maintain the throne:
I've fought for thee, for thee I still must fight,
To win a dawn o'er thy dishonoured night."

"'Twere kinder far," the lady sighed, "if thou
One little message from me wouldst allow:
Tell but my son his mother pines in thrall,
And win his visit to this lonely hall.
Yes, yes, my brother, you will bring my son,
Never to leave me till my days be done;
And not by me, but Allah's power, made wise,
He'll join us in the Prophet's Paradise.

"But let me not be selfish: stands not there
A wounded captive, by thy special care
Brought me to heal? Come near," she softly said,
Turning to Julian; "can I give thee aid?
Thou weep'st: Ah yes! thy mother dwells afar,
And little sisters ask thee back from war;
Gay vests they sew for thee, much-loved; and still
To look for thee they climb the green cleft hill,
From morn to noon they look, they watch for thee
Till gleams the sweet moon through the chestnut-tree.
But weep not: Allah bless my balms for pain,
And thou shalt see thy mother's home again!"

Why wept young Julian? He could only tell
Not for himself his tears, but for that Lady, fell;
Since first her look, her voice, had made him start,
And waked a thousand memories in his heart.

"His mother's home is here; lo! he's the same,
And none but he, that from thy body came:
Look to him, Zara; know'st thou not thy son?
But to our Prophet's faith he must be won."

Zemberbo thus. Forth springing, she made bare
The Captive's neck; she found, she kissed it there,
The mark, remembered long. Her hand she laid
Soft on his shoulder, and his face surveyed.
Faint in her joy she murmured:—"O my son!
My long-lost child, but now my dear found one!
Thou'rt come at last to bid my griefs be o'er,
And live with me, and never leave me more?
But oh, these rags, what mean they? must I, too,

Of sorrows ask, and sufferings borne by you?
But they are past. Sit here, my boy, and see
The better fortune I had shaped for thee!"

She said, and, having led him to a seat,
Unrolled a silken web before his feet,
Wrought of fine needlework, and showed thereon
—Her smile the while appealing to her son—
A gallant warrior in a princely garb,
Before ten thousand bounding on his barb.
High looked his eye and far, as doth a king's,
Who proudly home his conquering army brings.
He in the van: behind, his thousands came;
Instinct each soldier with his leader's fame,
Beyond his own, with double ardour trode;
Wide flung the uplifted spears their sheen abroad;
Shone banners terrible; and trumpets high
The whole attempered with dread harmony.
One spirit ruled the whole: So prompt to dare,
The wingèd triumph seemed to rise in air.
But blind to all beside, to him alone
That mother pointed in the van who shone.
And lo! the wonders of a mother's heart,
Which to her hand could thus her love impart—
So hoarded well—so lost not through the tide
Of long, long years—so to her work supplied:
True to the dear and unforgotten face,
Her long-lost boy's, her soul had known to trace
The beauteous copy from his childhood fair;
And Julian smiled to see his features there.
Nor less she smiled through tears of conscious joy,
And scanned his face:—"'Twere true, my princely boy,
But for vile cares which mar thee, and which we
Ne'er thought entitled in our work to be;
From which alone we failed thy face to know,
And, if not told, unclaimed had let thee go.
Well hast thou done, my heart, well hast thou done!
Say this for me, my unforgotten son!
Declare for me! and in this thing behold
A mother's love to work a dream of old!"

Why bursts not forth the Captive's heart to bless
Such love entire? New fears his heart repress.
There on the precious web he saw inwrought
With love's device for him a perilous thought;
His imaged form in Moslem robes was drest,
A caftan blue flowed o'er his linen vest,
And round his brow the turban's deep green fold

The princely lineage of the Prophet told:
So by this sign he feared his mother now
Earnest would have him to the Prophet bow.
Nor from that mother could his gloom be hid,
And thus his fears unguessed she fondly chid:—
"No more of this! Are not those dark days gone?
And all thy sorrows vanished with my own?
And now this hand, which wrought that cloth, must take
Its pattern thence, and garments for thee make,—
The turban first; oh, let me wreathe it now
Divinely green, my son, around thy brow!
To thee, to me, one faith, one hope be given;
And I'll not miss thee in the Prophet's Heaven!"

Dark waxed the Captive's face, as fixedly there
He stood, nor answered to his mother's prayer;
Far turned his eye, as if he could not brook
The silent pleading of a mother's look.
Her, sudden trembling seized: Around she glanced,
As if to see some danger new advanced;
Zemberbo's frowning brows her bosom fill
With dread, and thus she wails the anticipated ill:—
"So then, my son must go, and I be left
A desolate thing, how utterly bereft!"

"I will not go! My mother! look to me!"
That son exclaimed. "Might I but live with thee!
What shall I say? what do? For thy dear sake,
All bonds, save of dishonour, would I take!
For in my heart and soul I hold thee one
To claim the noblest service of a son!"

"Go on, Sir Youth! Swear," said Zemberbo, "Swear
By Allah she is worthy of all care.
Were she the pure as once I knew her pure,
High should she sit, nor darksome days endure;
Above ten crowns, a boast, a joy to me,
Above all price my bosom's twin should be!
But for that she was pure, and is not now,
The Prophet holds my high recorded vow,
To do my vengeance on thy father-king
Who dared to shame my Lilla Zara bring.
Captived and wounded when a Prince he lay
In Zemra's Palace: there his life away
Was ebbing fast; but there my sister dwelt
The while, and pity for his youth she felt.
Each precious bleeding rind, she knew its power,
And every virtual plant, and every sovereign flower

Beneath the moon; and how to win them knew,
On Atlas gathered in their nightly dew.

And to their powers she joined a spell of might
(The moon consenting, and the stars of night);
And Allah blessed her work of sweet young ruth,
And up from death she raised thy father's youth.
Now what for Lilla Zara shall be done?
How shall he grateful be to his redeeming one?
He tempted her; she fled with him by night,
And in his kingdom showed her tarnished light.
Well, style it love (omnipotent, they say):
What then? You deem not his could pass away?
His father dead, 'twas his to mount the throne;
Now then we'll see him glad his faithful one to own!
Dog in his heart, he sate thereon; but she,
How worthless now, no mate for him must be!
Forsooth! no doubt! her glory he desired,
But other queen his kingdom's wants required;
And thus, although my sister was his spouse,
His priests of Rome dissolved his marriage vows,
Divorcing them; and thus it was decreed
By policy that she must be a weed,
Cast out and trampled down! From Portugal
I swept her hither to this sunless thrall,
But missed her only boy: From blushing day
Here have I kept her hid, here shall she stay
Till with thy father's blood I wash her shame away.
For Fez I fought, but for my sister more,
To slay thy sire, or take him: for I swore,
Could I so take him living, to complete
My vengeance, with his blood I'd wash her feet.
Even should she die, embalmed unburied, she
Shall wait the chance, washed with his blood to be.
But now, for thee, Sir Captive:—Hither sent,
I meant to follow thee, my spirit bent
To change thy faith, to keep thee dwelling here,
Thy mother Zara in her bonds to cheer,
Till I should do my vengeance; in my mind
Respect for thee and power were then designed,
Thy mother lifted with thee. But the King
Thus far has turned my purpose on the wing,
That I will smite him too who spurned my will,
In thee thus fettered, and insults me still,
And hunts my life: For this, from off his throne
Down will I hurl him, and I'll sit thereon.
Then, when my vengeance is fulfilled, with me
High shall thy mother sit, and happy shall she be;

Thou, for her sake, the man of my right hand,
Honour shalt have, and place, and wide command.
But mark, Sir Captive, this:—The Prophet's faith
Here must thou take, or thou must die the death.
Thy father's blood that's in thee must be spilt,
Unless our Islam change its native guilt.
Thy mother's blood that's in thee must not live,
The lie degenerate to its font to give:
What! shall the blood that's of the Prophet's seed,
Maintain a traitor to the Prophet's creed?
So for your father's, for your mother's sake,
Perish you must, unless our faith you take.
Brief now: behold your mother: live or die:
You know the terms: we wait for your reply."

"Now, now, dear mother, deem me not unkind,"
The Captive said; "but bear it in thy mind,
That I have loved thee with a soul which scorned
The fears of death, not yielding to be turned
To bribed apostasy—oh, tempting sin,
The bribe thy presence, and my joy therein!
Nor wilt thou change thy faith. But yet one Lord,
Though differently by us on earth adored,
May mildly judge us, to one Heaven may save
Our souls, when we shall rise from out the grave.
So hope, so bear thou up. Give her relief,
Sweet Christ; I cannot live and look upon her grief!"

"Ho, guards!" Zemberbo cried. They came and bound
The Captive's eyes anew, and bore him from the ground.
Then, oh he felt, as he was borne away,
His mother's clinging kiss, which drew his heart to stay.
Torn from her grasp, he heard her struggling plaint,
As sore bereaved she fought against restraint;
How wished by him unheard! "Off! let me free!
Save me, my boy! Come back! Oh, come and be
A young believer for thy mother's sake!
Stay, stay, and teach me then thy faith to take,
That I may come unto thy Paradise;
My heart so longs to have thee in the skies!"

II.

Forth borne, and onward through the breathing night,
Freedom was given to Julian's limbs and sight.
Within the city wall the party stood,
A stream in front, behind a scattered wood.

The skirring moon flew on her shining track,
And from her horn-tips tossed the wispy rack,
Boring the West; o'er snowy Atlas high,
Ranged through the clearness of the southern sky,
With lengthened beams the stars told morn was nigh.
"Disperse, disguise ye, shun that vengeful King,"
Bespoke the Chief his guards; "you know the spring
Beyond the northern wall? I'll wait you there:
Steal through the various gates: once more, Beware!
Away! away! this youth shall be my care."

They went. To Julian said the Chief: "We spare thee
For one test more; let time and thought prepare thee:
O'er Fez we'll ride; we hold thee in our power,
To deal with thee in that decisive hour.
Come on with me; beyond the tyrant's thrall
This stream shall sweep us, issuing 'neath yon wall.
But ha! what's this?" For glimpsing points of mail,
Seen through the trees, his startled eyes assail.
Armed guards came on:—"Yield to thy King; prepare,
Sir Chief, thy bloody outrage to declare!"
They cried. Forth flashed Zemberbo's scimitar,
And on the foremost fell its edge of war
With sharing gash; and through a second fast,
And through a third, the shearing vengeance passed;
Still met the hemming foe with savage haste,
And shed defiance far and killing waste.
Like fire-scrolled parchments, shrunk his shag lips round,
Baring his ivory teeth that fiercely ground;
Heaved his wide nostril with disdainful ire;
Shook his black locks; gleamed his great eye of fire;
Swept his unbaffled arm: with many a stride
Far-shifting, sped his work from side to side,
Till, pressed by numbers, in the stream he dashed,
A moment sank, then rose, and fiercely flashed
Above the breasted billows, highly waved
His dripping sword, and thus the danger braved:—
"Caitiffs, we yet shall meet! yea, tell your King,
Of bloody sabres shall we presents bring.
High on his turrets watching, let him see
Our coming-on, which gloriously shall be
By lights of burning towns—wild measuring line,
O'er hill and valley shall it stretch and shine!
Now for the lantern of yon imaged moon,
To guide us forth: vengeance—we'll have it soon!"
He said, and down into the waters went;
They gurgled round him, nor his reascent
His watchful foes could see. But hark! that shout

Beyond the wall: the stream has borne him out.

III.

And to his shout, thrice with his scimitar
Zemberbo smote the wall, the earnest of his war.
Yet not his soul indignant was content
Till, fear-defying, to the gates he went,
And smote them too. Then northward, swift of foot,
He ran, lest mounted foes were in pursuit;
Rough hills in view, there he can hide a space
From foes pursuing, and defy their chase.
But lo! comes on a stranger on his barb,
Through the dim dawn, of Moorish front and garb.
Stood in his path Zemberbo, questioned high
Of name and place, and claimed a prompt reply.
"A friend to Fez; and tidings for the King,"
The horseman said, "but death for thee we bring,
If thus you dare our onward way to bar:
Give place, and shun our weightier scimitar."
"Friend to the tyrant? perish for that word!"
Zemberbo cried, struck down the stranger's sword,
Disarmed him, smote again, and hewed away
His turbaned head, far rolling in the clay.
Plunged the chafed charger; from the quivering trunk
Forth spun the purple life-strings, ere it sunk;
Nor sunk it yet, but sate a hideous sight,
And still it held the reins with hands convulsed and white,
Till, tumbled by the victor from its place,
He sate instead, and urged his vehement pace.

And on, fast, far he flew; nor scorned to bless
The gallant steed, whose speed was only less
Than his winged heart indignant: He caressed
The tossing mane that swept his urging breast,
And toyed with it in the fierce dallying play
Of spirit burning for a boundless sway.
But turning oft, the Fezzan towers he cursed.
Up the steep ways he strained, down on the vales he burst,
Devoured the plain, and swam the rapid stream,
And shook its coldness from him like a dream.
Uprose the sun; straight through a dowar's ground
The Chieftain rode, disdaining to go round;
Brushed down the crashing tents, nor stayed to hear
The awakened sleepers with their cries of fear.
Noon passed: eve came: he saw the rushing sea,
In great accordance with his energy.

Then by the tawny sands Zemberbo went,
And reached his camp, and rested in his tent.

CANTO IV.

THE BATTLE.

Who sent those armèd men to seize or slaughter
Zemberbo, scarce escaping by the water?
The Monarch sent them. Reached by those alarms
Of midnight outrage and Zemberbo's arms,
Startled he stood. Zenone came and threw
Over the whole her own convenient hue:
Zemberbo (thus deceptive she explained),
His heart still gloomy for his kinsman chained,
With many a threat of his vindictive ire
Had roused the loyal city; they with fire
Had striven to burn him, that he ne'er might go
To do his vengeance as a traitor foe;
But they had failed. It gave the Monarch cheer
Thus of his city's loyalty to hear;
But still he feared the baited Chief; and still
His rising wish was him at once to kill,
Could it be done: The Monarch long revolved
The growing purpose, and at length resolved:—
"His death's our only safety; die this hour
Zemberbo must, while yet he's in our power."
Zenone wished not this; not hers to slay
The instrument of her avenging day,
Coming apace: She pled, but pled in vain
To spare the Chief—the King will have him slain.
At every gate and outlet of the town
Prompt guards were placed to cut the rebel down,
Nor let him pass. Found by that armèd band,
Zemberbo smote them till his weary hand
Could smite no more; unequal to them all,
Plunging he took the stream, and 'scaped beneath the wall.

II.

Unfettered, scathless from that midnight fray,
Back to the Palace Julian made his way;
Zemberbo's plans rebellious he declared,
And bade the Monarch be for war prepared.
The war came on: So great Zemberbo's sway,

He from their fealty drew his camp away.
Yet well to be opposed; so many kings
To his defence the Fezzan Monarch brings,
So many chiefs, so many princes: They
Zemberbo's power and traitorous array,
A bad example, fearing, deem it now
The time to check him, nor his growth allow.
And Julian joins them: for his mother's sake,
That her from darkness he to light may take,
Oh how he longs Zemberbo's power to break!
And for his father's, that the Chieftain's wrath
No more may plague him and contrive his death!
And for his Geraldine's not less, that she
With ruined Fez may not a victim be!
He sent his sire a message, stating all
That had befallen him in his captive thrall;
And praying him to watch the coming fight,
And send a squadron of reservèd might,
To turn the battle and Zemberbo smite;
But not himself to lead it on, that so
Safe he might keep from his inveterate foe.
Should they Zemberbo quell, to Portugal
Her old demands shall be conceded all—
So sware the Fezzan King; and Geraldine,
Pledge of the friendly peace, O Julian, shall be thine.

III.

"And fear not, weep not, Love!" thus fondly said
The Captive's farewell to his Moorish maid,
As in the sweetness of the twilight hour
They sate together in a garden bower:
'Twas ere he went to battle. "Down amain
If we Zemberbo smite, to thee again
I'll come; and I will take thee from this shore,
Light of my life! the dark-blue waters o'er,
To banks of beauty, where the Tagus roves
Through the long summer of his orange groves.
And when thou turn'st thee to the southern star,
And think'st upon thy native home afar,
Thou shalt not weep; I have thee by the hand,
My heart is thine, my land shall be thy land.
I feel, I feel my love's unbounded debt!
May God forget me when I thee forget!"

"No, no," said Geraldine; "it must not be!
Risk not the fight, come not again to me!

My sisters, and my brother, who but I
Must watch them for our mother in the sky?
She bade me love them well, she bade me make them
The lambs of Christ; how then can I forsake them?
Yet in this hour I'll say it,—dear, O Youth,
Art thou to me for thy heroic truth,
Far more than thrones, and crowns, and kingly brows!
Sweet Prince, beyond what female grace allows,
Think me not light and bold; but all my life
I'd love to be thy true and faithful wife.
It cannot be. But hark!" She softly said,
And to her Julian bent her beauteous head.
Was it to whisper? Or his cheek to touch
With hers so soft? How little, yet how much!
'Twas nature's holy kiss! No sooner paid,
Than forth away she flitted through the shade.

IV.

Uprose the sun: By Rasalema's side,
The Fezzan river, moved in martial pride
A mingled host from various realms, to stem
Zemberbo's treason, and the diadem
Maintain of Abusade: in rank and square
Swarming they join, and for the march prepare.

Loud blew a thousand trumpets; deep and high
Was filled the compass of war's harmony,
Attempered terrible: thrilling it shook
The soldier's heart, and raised his daring look.
Outflew a thousand banners. And the mass
Of moving valour shook the valley pass
With sounding tread. From the high walls behind
Of Fez came shouts upon the morning wind;
There myriads stood, and bade their army on
To conquer for the city and the throne.
So shall they conquer! How shall be subdued
The embodied kingdoms' warlike multitude?
Puffed yellow Copts are here, and soldiers brave
From Nubian hill and Abyssinian cave.
The unshadowed lands, that hear each sultry noon
The thunders 'yond the Mountains of the Moon,
Have sent a few bold men; but many a swarm
Gives Negroland, scarce less the dusk and warm.
Fierce kingdoms on the west to Ocean's brink,
And they whose horses the far waters drink
Of Syrian streams, have men enlisted here.

The warlike Berbers from the hills more near
Of crescent Atlas and the vales between,
The blameless Shelluhs, and the aspects keen
Of mountain Errifi, and Hea's wild castes,
That scream like eagles on the lofty blasts,
March on to battle. Lo! the army's pride,
The Hentets on their fine-haired horses ride;
With hordes unnumbered from the lesser states
Of Atlas southward to the Land of Dates.
From Tremecen, Azogue, Zenhagian, Hoar,
And Heneti, brave tribes that hunt the boar
Far in the gorges of the snowy hills,
Whose glossy range its southern border fills,
Or roam wild Angab's desert to the banks
Of soft Moluya, fill the Fezzan ranks.
Two days they marched; the third beheld them stayed:
Their fair encampment in a vale was made.
Beyond it lay, a narrow pass between,
A larger valley, and an equal scene
Of martial pomp; for there the traitor host
Of dark Zemberbo kept their evening post,
And hoped the coming morn. Not less possest
Of hope, the Royal army took their rest.
By heaven and earth! it was a goodly sight
To see their tents beneath the setting light,
Encircling with their white pavilioned pale
A little hill mid rising in the vale.
Cedars and palms, with sunlight in their tops,
In leafy tiers grew up its gentle slopes.
Green was its open head, there walked or sate
The Captains and the Kings confederate.
West through the vale delicious lay unrolled
The lapse of rivers in their evening gold,
While far along their sun-illumined banks
Broke the quick restless gleam of warlike ranks.
North, where the hills arose by soft degrees,
Stood stately warriors in the myrtle-trees,
And fed their beauteous steeds. From east to south
Armed files stood onward to the valley's mouth.
From out the tents the while, and round the plain,
Bold music burst defiance to maintain,
And hope against the morrow's dawning hour.
Nor the gay camp belied the inspiring power:
From white-teethed tribes, that loitered on the grass,
Loud laughter burst, fierce jests were heard to pass;
Around the tents were poured the gorgeous throngs
Of nations blent, with shouts and martial songs.
Nor ceased the din as o'er the encampment wide

Fell softly dark that eve of summer-tide.

V.

Gray morn appeared. "My horse!" Zemberbo cried;
And forth was brought, shrill-neighing in his pride,
His battle-horse—from Araby a gift,
White as the snows, and as the breezes swift:
A chosen foal, on Yemen's barley fed,
In size and beauty grew the desert-bred,
Fit present for a King: his burnished chest,
Branched o'er with veins, and muscles ne'er at rest,
Starts, throbs, and leaps with life; his eyeballs glow;
Quick blasts of smoke his tender nostrils blow.
The Chieftain sprung on him. The rolling drum
Announced his signal that the hour was come
His men should move: Trumpet and deep-smote gong
Quell to the draining march the closing throng.
On through the short defile, compact and slow,
Betwixt the vales, Zemberbo's squadrons go.
Lo! the King's host. The mutual armies seen,
Fierce shouts arose, and claimed the space between.
Paused not the rebel phalanx: On each hand
Hung cloudy swarms, whence, ranging in a band,
The stepping archers, with their pause compressed,
Let loose the glancing arrows from their breast.
Nor less from loyal bows the arrowy rain
Dark on the advancing column fell amain,
Advancing still: in crescent-shaped array,
The Fezzan host in its embosomed bay
Receives it deep; but sharpens round away,
Till curling to the column's flanks it turns,
And turning bores them with its piercing horns.
Yet onward still, still onward through the fight,
That column pushed its firm continuous might,
Till, widening out, it spread a breastwork far
Across the plain, and mingled deep the war.

But where is Julian? At the break of day
Came on his father with a bold array,
Brought by the message of his son; but fear
Disdaining for himself, himself is here
Leading his warriors on, sooner to bar
Zemberbo's rise, and end a long-protracted war.
Oh how rejoicing to his native band
Did Julian leap! His father, hand in hand
He'll fight with him! And, through that stormy day,

They crossed Zemberbo in his fellest way.
Faint toiled the staggering battle. Fresh and strong,
A giant troop came dashingly along,
Grim set, reserved for this: Lo! bare of head,
The black compacted turm Zemberbo led;
Low couching, forward bent: and stern and still,
His sword intensely waited on his will,
Held pointed by his side. Across his path
Resistance came, and eased his rigid wrath,
Which bowed him corded down: How towering rose
The mighty creature, and made shreds of foes;
His face, as far he bounded to destroy,
Bright with the sunshine of his warlike joy!
He pointed to the thickest of the fight,
There fought the King of Portugal, with might
There Julian fought; deep plunged into the fray
That sable corps, and cleared the crush away;
Then, with the stress of numbers hemming round
That King, they bore him from the embattled ground,
And bore his son; but not one wounding blade
Was dealt on them, for so Zemberbo bade:
Thus Julian and his sire were captive made.
Their capture smote with fear the Fezzan host;
It paused, it wavered, turned, fled—all was lost.

VI.

"Oh for our warriors back!" young Geraldine
Stood on her Palace at the day's decline,
And longing thus she sighed. Far looking forth,
She saw a coming from the purple north.
Behind in Fez a buzzing murmur rose,
Like as of men presentient of their woes;
For there's a sharpness, not of ear or eye,
Which tells to waiting realms of ruin nigh,
A sense prophetic: not one fugitive
Was yet come in the evil news to give;
Yet seemed o'er Fez the air instinct with ills,
Seemed running whispers over all her hills.
To cries of fear they waxed, and crowds amain
Stood on their roofs and looked unto the plain:
There now they come, in straggling disarray,
The weary relics of some fatal day:
Far bends the rider o'er his staggering steed,
And scarcely seems the expected walls to heed,
Scarce lifts his feeble eyes: each man alone
In deep unsocial stress of mind comes on.

Forth going, thousands meet them; thousands wait
To bid them welcome at each friendly gate;
In anxious silence thousands look and long
To find their kin in that returning throng.
Absorbed in fear stood Geraldine, and viewed
With dizzy eyes the thickening multitude.

Night fell: she listened: swelling from afar
Came music on, as of triumphant war.
It ceased: how throbbed her bosom, half relieved
To think her ear had haply been deceived!
But oh yon moving lights! and oh the tread
Of marching squadrons, deep, concentrated!
And tinklings of the horse! Cries of command,
Distinctly heard, proclaim the foe at hand,
Heard round from post to post; the points of light
Glance to and fro, and widen through the night;
The solid tread is fused to swarming din
Of men who nightly bivouac begin.
"Zemberbo's camp! Ah me!" the damsel sighed,
And to her chamber through the darkness hied.

CANTO V.

THE FIRE.

Behold Zenone, as she sits by night,
All pale and pensive, robed in virgin white!
Her chief of eunuchs came; absorbed in thought,
Her eyes she raised not, and she saw him not.
But Melki bowed and kissed her silken feet,
Raised back his withered brow her eye to meet,
Then seized her hand. She started: "Slave!" she said,
"I know thee faithful, but I'm past thy aid.
Why com'st thou, then? Away! I love thee not,
And little have I done to cheer thy luckless lot."

"Italian flower!" upstarting said the slave,
"The land that gave thee birth to me my being gave!
I'd have thee be a Queen magnificent!
Like bow, to serve thee, is my spirit bent!
To our own Italy we'll turn."

"No, no!"
Zenone sighed: "How could I thither go?
In that fair land first lightened on my eyes

The suns of summer from the crystal skies.
How fair and glad! But glad to me no more!
The ghosts would meet me on the dreary shore!
I see the flames! I hear my mother's cry!
Is this a monstrous dream? Where, what am I?
Why should I live? Oh let me die away!
Love, Pride, Ambition, Power, so perish they.
Even boasted Genius, Heaven-endowed to raise
The young religion of man's primal days,
When Virtue was an ardour, not a thing
To wait on Habit for a tutored wing,
By Passion maddened, worse than doomed to die,
How oft it turns its glory to a lie!
What then is life, if thus the goodliest fall?
Cease, my vexed soul, 'tis vain delusion all!"

"So give us active joys, nor let us waste
Our heart in dreams; but plan and do in haste:"
The eunuch said. Zenone answered this:—
"Ha! think'st thou, slave, that aught shall make me miss
The only triumph that can be my bliss?
No: I shall come before a nation's eyes;
Fez, she may curse me, she shall ne'er despise.
I to her painted roll my name refuse,
Of spotted harlots in these silken stews;
Yet shall that name in Fez be ne'er forgot,
But stamp her annals with a burning blot.
Come on, Zemberbo, thou art linked with me;
Careering twins in vengeance shall we be!"

"He's come; he's here: our army smitten down,"
The eunuch said, "this night he'll shake our town;
But strong, defended well, Morocco near
In arms to thwart him in preventive fear,
And aid our King, though doomed, yet still it may
For many a moon stave off the evil day."

Up springs Zenone; o'er her countenance pass,
In flamings like a chemist's kindled glass,
The varying passions. Settled, pale, and still,
A deadly whisper thus declared her will:—
"My hour is come! We'll let Zemberbo in,
And do the rest! Come on with me! No din!
Tread softly, Child! Hark! of my mortal cup
The King shall drink, 'twill dry his spirit up;
Then to his roof let him be carried, there
To win the coolness of the freer air;
When round him there his children gathered be,

My fire shall catch them, nor shall let them flee:
My father's house and lineage to the flame
He dared to give, I'll do for him the same,
Far then we'll go. But come, my inner room
Must better fit us for our work of doom."

She said, and going in her stern intent
Locked up and pale, behind her Melki went.

II.

O'er Fez triumphant, with embattled din
Zemberbo rode: Zenone let him in,
Through Melki's aid: His grizzly aspect gleamed,
Far o'er his head his coal-black banner streamed.
Forth rushed his ruffian hordes, all kindred ties
Long distant wars had taught them to despise.
What shouts afar! What shriekings of affright!
And sound of steeds that galloped through the night!

Blaze followed blaze till, one unbroken glare,
Wide o'er the city burned the midnight air.
Chased by the gleam of swords, a wildered throng
From street to street with shrieks were driven along,
With wild back-streaming looks, unmarried maids,
And mothers glaring through the umbered shades,
With clasping babes, and crooked forms of eld
That feebly plained, and by the younger held.
Blood bubbling flowed, and every deed of shame
Was done that links to Hell man's boasted name.

On rode Zemberbo to the central square
Of Fez: The King of Portugal was there,
Brought near his Julian; firm, in governed mood,
Beside his sorrowing son the Monarch stood.
"Why are you here, my father? Do you know
The things prepared against you by that foe?"
Thus Julian spake: "Dark Chieftain on thy steed,
Say, can a gallant soldier have decreed
A King like this should live with shackled arms?
Why, do but honour to the old alarms
Of mutual war, to him that aye was found
A worthy foe, and let him stand unbound."

"No change of bonds," Zemberbo said, "he'll find,
Till the stark cordage of the grave shall bind
His head, his heart; beyond the purple hour

When o'er an Arab's feet his blood he'll pour.
That hour is now at hand: No wish of mine
E'er perished: Allah, be the glory thine!
So learn, Sir Youth, to hold thee humble still,
Nor rashly try to thwart my conquering will."

"Spare him!" cried Julian. "Me, strike home on me,
If for our blood thy soul must thirsty be.
He speaks, dear father, of my mother's feet;
And oh, I fear his scheme he can complete!"

"Now, now," that father said, "'tis mine to press
Thy heart, my son, for great forgiveness!
Yet her I loved: I only was not bold,
Against my people,s wish, my marriage to uphold.
So was she lost. And oh, a father's shame!
Scarce have I dared to tell you of her name.
Yet for her sake, methinks, my love for you
Has been, if possible, above your due.
I know my doom, our captor has explained;
Yet trust I then his wrath shall be restrained,
Nor farther work against thy youth, but break
Thy galling fetters for thy mother's sake."

"Now is the crisis! now the last dread hour,"
Zemberbo said, "to bend him to my power!
For this, Sir King, I've led thee forth to meet
Thy Captive son, that thou with him may'st treat,
May'st change his faith, that him I here may make
A prince and chieftain for his mother's sake.
Much has he dared against me; yet I still,
More than forgiving, shall these terms fulfil,
So thou wilt change his creed. Else, sworn have I,
A doom abides him sterner than to die."

The King, he spake not; but he stood a space,
How wistful, looking in his Julian's face.

"My father!" Julian said, "thy love for me
Is broad, and deep, and pure as pure can be!
Fain wouldst thou have me saved; yet well I know
Thy soul would have me ne'er my faith forego.
Ne'er shall it be. Oh, I have dared deny
My mother's heart, and left her lone to die!
Say now—'tis come to this—well are we met,
Ere go we each to pay his bloody debt."

"Give me, my son, the proud young martyr's kiss:

For faith be flint: fear nothing: faith is bliss."

So said that father; and the loyal youth
Impressed the solemn kiss, his pledge of truth.
High stood the King, and spake:—"Rise, Son of Heaven!
Ride in thy chariot: terrible be it driven!
Go forth—go down upon thy foes, and break
The billow of thy wheels on Mahomet's neck!"

Dark, darker waxed Zemberbo; but he sate
Silent, his sister's coming to await,
By him commanded hither: Lives she yet?
Or has her day of many sorrows set,
Twice severed from her son? He raised his head,
Startled; there came a litter for the dead.
"Allah! my sister!" groaned the sable Chief,
And ground his teeth to check his softer grief.
Down from his charger springing, lowly bowed
He met the body; 'neath a linen shroud
Embalmed it lay. Brief question asked, he bade
The litter near the captive King be stayed.
Then, "Hear me, see me, judge me, Chiefs!" exclaimed
Zemberbo, turning to his Captains famed:
"I had a sister once; ye knew her shame,—
Her hateful marriage, her dishonoured name:
Stand forth who deems my wrath was then unmoved;
Or—is there such?—that I her love approved;
Or—where is he?—that vengeance I've forgot;
Behold the triumph of my treasured thought:
Ne'er has it slept: My heart was only slow,
The better to secure this deepest blow."
He said, and turning with a mighty stride,
Drove down into the patient Monarch's side
His steel vindictive; from their snowy sheet
Baring his sister's fixed and bony feet,
O'er them he held the faint sustainèd King,
To rain his blood thereon, reeking from life's red spring.

"Ho! double vengeance! be the banner brought,
Last from him ta'en!" And to Zemberbo's thought
In wrath refining, and his stern command,
The rustling flag was lowered to his hand;
He wiped her bloody feet with it, and drew
The folds of linen over them anew.

O Julian, then! A flash sprang o'er his eyes,
As high he saw that eager weapon rise;
With short quick cry he turned him as it fell,

And shrunk to hear it glut itself so well;
With panting breast, he saw the foe fulfil
The fearful process of his vengeful will;
Till, by Zemberbo's grasp no more upstayed,
The bleeding Monarch in the dust was laid.
He sprung, he sprung, his father's hand to press,
To kneel, to whisper, and his head to bless;
Till death-divided was their mutual kiss.
He closed his father's eyes; without a tear,
Stately he stood in dignity severe.

Near bursts a sudden glare! Through all its frame
The Palace burns in one consuming flame.
But see the lovely Fury! Still the brand
Which did the deed is in Zenone's hand.
How shines the creature's face! But to the ground
A camel kneels; she mounts it with a bound,
And rising, glimpsing flees; behind her near,
Through every peril, and through every fear,
To go with her, each toil, each wo to brave,
Another camel bears her eunuch slave.
From land to land she went; but frenzied Pain,
Fell dog, pursued and overtook her brain,
And bayed her down: Down into Etna's tide
Of lava plunged she: this her dying pride,
That the pure fire should be her burial-place,
Nor her heart rot with man's ignoble race.

The Fezzan Palace burns. On every side
The ragged web of flame is wafted wide;
Back drawn, it clings, it climbs, updarting oft
Its far-thrust tongues that curl and lick aloft
All round the roof, still curling inward. There
The poisoned King is dying in his chair:
Zenone's scheme. Young Geraldine is seen
Bathing his brow, with many a kiss between.
His other children—see the dear young band!
Round him they hang, and hold him by the hand.
Urged by the heat, they shrink, they hide their eyes,
They press upon his breast their stifled cries.

One wrench, and Julian's free: One mighty bound
Has borne him clear beyond that guarded ground.
Yon lovely family from the fire he'll save,
Or die with them in one devouring grave!
He nears the Palace, dashing in he dares
The flames—Christ help him now to climb the burning stairs!
A fearful pause! Oh, on the roof he springs,

His arms around his Geraldine he flings,
To bear her thence: one kiss upon her brow—
The pillars crack, the blazing rafters bow,
Down goes the roof, the walls down inward go;
A smoking, smothered mass of ruin glares below!
But where are they whom scarce the twinking eye
Has ceased to see upon that Palace high?
Whelmed in its wreck their mingled ashes lie.
Disturb them not! Of Julian only tell,
He died with her whom he had loved so well.